One Warrior To Another

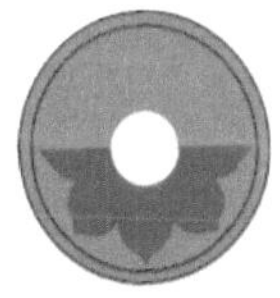

One Warrior to Another

"Brother, you're not alone."

A Vietnam Combat Veteran's Reflection

Richard Cleaves

atmosphere press

For my children:
Mary Jo
Katie
Mathew
Philip

Contents

Foreword
by Richard's brother

This is my brother's story. That is to say, he wrote it; it's not a story about him. He frequently consulted our sister for practical and spiritual advice. Originally called "My Sister Said", this little missive is dedicated in spirit to her.

We were three siblings. My brother Richard was the oldest, Lorraine was next, and I'm the baby. The family grew up and bonded in the Willard section of South Portland, Maine. Even though we all left after high school, our collective hearts will always be at our beach. Willard Beach was the gathering area for hundreds of people in our world, but still my family will always say it was "our" beach.

Let's start off with a little math. My brother lived on this earth for a total of 25,509 days. The first 7,876 included childhood, school, college, marriage, entrance into the Army, and generally growing up in southern Maine.

Then, Vietnam.

For roughly 365 days, he was a boat mechanic, gunner, sniper, and boat captain for the Army Riverine forces on the Mekong Delta.

He came home a different man. Our mother noticed this on his first night home; she said, "They took my son and sent back someone else."

She knew.

This was coming from a woman who saw her husband, brother, and uncles head off to WWII action. She instinctively knew Vietnam was a different type of war. It chewed up young men and spit them out with no apologies.

My brother went from horror to home in a few days. Our father had months to decompress from Europe to America after WWII.

One evening, shortly after he returned, I asked what any little brother might ask. I wanted to know about his experiences. All I got were a few mumbles and the infamous thousand-yard stare, popularized by *Life* magazine correspondent Tom Lea. I just needed to share my older brother's experiences during the most intense year of his life. He just wanted to forget.

More than forget, erase.

That one year was the most transformative and psychologically oppressive year imaginable. Exactly how does one defeat a memory?

It wasn't simply memories. He traversed the gamut, from idyllic life to horror, back to idyllic life again. The transitions were more than he could handle.

This short book is about one man's experience. And, he would want me to express his love and admiration for all first responders and those who serve in our five branches of the military.

My brother started this book while in the New Mexico VA Health Care System. A therapy mechanism, his doctors said. This is his attempt at coming back to life. He came close but was constantly haunted for the remaining 17,269 days of his life.

He taught himself gourmet cooking. It was over his wonderful creations we talked a lot about this story in general terms; he was never forthcoming with details. He asked me to wait until sometime after he left this earth to make sure this effort was made available.

I'd be unfair to the truth if I didn't say this: there were times he would put Emeril to shame (Have you ever had blueberry and sweet cream crepes? I thought not.); there were other times he couldn't make toast. Maybe that's brotherly competition, but I stayed away from his breads.

Ultimately, he succumbed to the chemical trauma and injuries he suffered in Vietnam. In fact, one VA doctor told him most men in his condition had already committed suicide. I was there.

However, he wouldn't leave such a legacy for his children and grandchildren. He refused to give in to total despair. In the end he survived; he endured. Since his homecoming in September 1969, he wrestled with the demons every day. He was one of the many haunted who never really came home.

I remember the day he came home, he saved his first kiss for his eight-month-old daughter who he hadn't met, then his wife, then our mother. The rest of us were extra, and that's only proper.

Everything in the bulk of this book is just as Richard wrote it. Not one word was changed in the editing. He was my big brother, my hero, and my mentor.

He hated it when I said that, preferring to say, "I'm no hero." Through his trials he was obviously a stronger man than he allowed himself to be.

In his own words, please read:

My sister said, "It isn't fair."

Since she has been the keeper of my soul for many, many years, I have to wonder whether or not she is right or wrong. When my world fell apart, she was the one person who was able to keep me on course. Since God was my enemy, she became my only source of any chance of salvation: and not for passage to heaven; but for any chance to once again feel like I deserve to be alive.

Still Alive – Why?

Five, ten, sixteen, eighteen years;
Friends, brothers, sisters;
Good parents, and a good home.
All is well.
The future is bright and happy;
Innocent, happy and FREE.

Then, "Greetings" – My country has called.
Everything is green.
The days are long and hard.
Growing up is accelerated.
No more excuses;
The collision of life or Death has arrived.

A short trip through the sky;
It's hot and smells bad.
Boys become men with weapons of destruction.
We move with one mind.
Not sure of our mission;
Thinking of home and wondering "Why?"

The first collision of Life or Death;
For me this time – Life.
Again and again – Life – "Why?"
"Will I survive?" — Do I want to survive?"

One by one — gone:
Happiness is gone;
Love is gone;
Innocence is gone;
Thoughts of home are dangerous.

With only a black heart do we keep going.
Our feelings are encased in granite;
Save those of hate, rage, and helplessness.

Principle and morality are replaced by the need
to kill and maim
For those who have fallen.
"Still Alive – Why?"

Finally home.
A Hero's welcome? — "Oh no!"
For there are no Heroes of war;
Only the dead and the not — so — lucky.

Five, ten, twelve, sixteen, eighteen years more;
The block of granite still solid.
Confused and hurting; "Why has my country
forsaken me?"
For I love it so: "STILL ALIVE – WHY?"

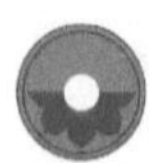

So if I pondered the idea of fair or not fair; I would have to question my patriotism, and that is not an option I am willing to entertain. My sons have not had to go to war – have yours? But I remember a son I encountered one night on the Mekong Delta:

Gone

Standing watch over a crew of five,
Surrounded by a warm blanket of darkness;
The river was quiet,
And I was alone.

Young in years he stepped out of the shadows,
His burden was one of death.
I watched as he came toward me.
His steps not heard over the pounding of my heart.

In less than a breath I took him into my arms;
My knife was swift and true;
His soul was gone;
But safe was my crew.

My palms warm against his body;
My arms cold in the silent black water;

Is it fair that my sons are spared the horror of war when other sons died at the hands of someone like me? I am torn with the answer to that question. Are you happy that this little boy died to spare your sons, daughters, brothers, or sisters?

I have often said that I wish I could be half the dad to my children that my dad was to me, but I fear that time is no longer on my side to help me with that goal. So writing from my heart to my children:

My Legacy

I am bound by a sense of rightness.
I have made my contribution to the restoration of freedom.

I am bound by a sense of loyalty. Thanks to the
help and support of
My fellow warriors, I have weathered the adversity
Of bombs and bullets – on and of the field of battle.

I am bound by a sense of reverence. I have seen my
comrades in arms
Felled by those same bombs and bullets. I have
etched upon my heart and mind
The faces of those who gave the ultimate sacrifice,
And pledge my honor and deeds to their memory.

Today I live in a land where freedom is a special
monument

*To who I am and what I stand for. Nowhere else in
the world
Is individual freedom so strongly embraced.
Nowhere else in the world
Is freedom more fully nurtured and allowed to
grow.*

*Please, God, if I leave nothing else in this world,
Let my children understand why I have done the
things I have done.
Let them feel the love I have for them. Give them
the strength to endure their trials of freedom.
Let them enjoy the wisdom of peace, and let them
respect the price of freedom.*

Since the writing of "My Legacy," my children have
married and given me seven grandchildren. My oldest
just giving birth to the youngest. Is it possible that they
will not have to go to war? The task of preserving the
peace, so many have paid for, is now left to those much
younger than I.

I pray that those of us who are left have given these warriors of peace the tools to be successful. Since our women are now able to fight for our freedom, I pray that my granddaughters will also not have to go to war. I remember a very young girl I encountered in the Mekong:

Eyes

> We stepped out of our boat
> To pursue the enemy.
> Cornering an old man
> Who was guarding his life with his
> granddaughter's
> I could not fire.
>
> He was put into chains;
> She into my care.
> So much fear in her eyes;
> So much trembling throughout her body.
>
> She was hungry, dirty and so tired.
> Did not understand that I was her friend;
> And could not understand my words;
> Nor me hers.

For her safety and comfort;
I turned her over to my native counterpart.
On their boat she went;
And darkness befell us;
And all was quiet.

Watching a clear and bright moon;
I heard laughter from this other boat;
Taking my crew to join in the festivities;
I was presented with yet another horror of war:

She was the party.

Picking up her bleeding,
Almost lifeless body;
My eyes gave the command to fire;
And her abusers were dead;
And their boat set adrift.

On my deck I placed her;
Could only stop some of her life-giving fluid
From staining my clothes and deck;
And our eyes fused in a stare
That will last for an eternity.

I do not know when her soul left this world
For her brown and round eyes never closed;
And those eyes so young
Will never leave my memory;
For I see them every waking moment.

Turning my back on God
Who could not be so loving

Fair? I am not sure. My mind can understand the wisdom of war, but my soul does not. My sister says so many wise and wonderful things. My brother is so solid and easygoing. My course in life has kept me from these two wonderful people, and because of that, I have spent many years wishing that that didn't have to be – not anymore! Where the man I always wanted to be is I am not sure, but much of that man can be seen in my sister and brother.

If my brother were asked whether or not to go to war, he might say something like: "If we are really in the pursuit of happiness, peace and freedom for all men and women, I would suggest that we settle our differences with a smile and not a gun." My sister might follow with: "I agree and God bless you."

Over the years I have longed to have my sister and brother very close to me, but I have missed that mark over and over again. When I think of how blessed I am to now have them as part of my life, I can't help but think of the brothers and sisters I deprived of ever seeing each other again. To take a life is, well, I will try to explain with:

That Millisecond

Through the crosshairs I see my target. My right hand holds this man-made invention of destruction firmly against my left shoulder. The muscles in my index finger slowly tighten, and my ears listen for the "click" which signals the departure of an ounce of lead: destined for the flesh of my "enemy".

A small explosion proceeds that familiar sound of steel hitting brass. The ignited gunpowder creates a gas, which builds in pressure to start this well-shaped piece of metal on its journey.

As the bullet passes the machined rifles in this tunnel of steel, it accelerates and moves quickly out of the way of the next pellet, which has the same destination.

The bullet cuts through the air and finds its mark. My enemy drops to the ground while his soul leaves his body. He will not live to be able to do what I have done in this milli-second. He will not see his family, his home, or another sunset.

His place is quickly taken by another of his kind – only to fall in the same way. Again and again my left index finger is challenged, and again and again it wins.

Silence is soon my comforter. This small space on this earth is shared by only those who were quicker and more lucky.

I have avoided "Death's" invitation this day, but I wonder why.

As I watch the red river of life ebb from my target's body, my heart becomes solid, and my soul becomes black.

"Why?"
"For what?"
"Could there have been a better way?"
"Where is the wisdom in all of this?"

These questions I asked myself then: these questions I continue to ask myself. These questions, I fear, have no answers.

Is it fair that I took the lives of other's brothers and sisters so that I might still have mine? I am not sure. Do you still have your brothers and sisters?

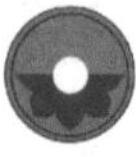

I still stand on common ground with my fellow combat soldiers. So many of us have given into our memories and ended their own lives. So many have kept on the move around this world. So many have lost their families. But I stand with no one would not do it all over again. Maybe, this time, you might help us if we should ever have to do it again – think so?

My sister says that all that is needed to follow the Ten Commandments is LOVE. But where is the Love she talks about? Is it a feeling? Is it a decision? Or is it something that only people like my sister and brother are allowed to have. Is it earned or given? Can it be found, lost and found again? Maybe Love is always present but ignored. And what of a mother's love – is there any other like theirs?

I thought I knew what love was when I married my seventh grade sweetheart, but whatever that feeling really was, I left on the field of battle. Three and a half decades later, I am still trying to figure out what my sister has been saying.

I will share with you how I am feeling this morning
about a lady I left last night.

Apart

Being together is so precious;
Loneliness overcomes me when we are not.
Sadness implants itself in my heart.
And my soul reaches for hers.

Our eyes see the same moon.
We see the same stars;
The same sunrise
And the same sunset;
But apart.

So as precious as being together can be;
So can being apart be precious;
For their no greater love,
Then that which has no boundaries.

Maybe our stars will fuse together.
Maybe that moon will become our home.
And maybe
Apart no more.

What I am feeling is as foreign to me as not being in combat. I have remained battle-ready for all these years, but for what? This lady says that life is lived one day at a time. And that everything happens in God's way and in His time. I am most definitely walking on ground that I may not have the right to walk on. I just don't know and will have to see what my sister says.

I know that until now, today, this minute, I have never placed anything above or regarded anything more important than that singular year I spent defending our country. So why now? I suspect that God has a great deal to do with whatever is going on in my heart. What do you think?

If you have not been in combat and not done or seen some of the things only a few warriors ever see, you might not understand this writing. If there is one thing I would say to my fellow Americans, it would be something I wrote for a speech I gave to the Apache Nation on Veteran's Day in 1991.

From One Warrior to Another

*Look at each other and feel the common bond.
This is a bond that cannot and will not be broken.
It is this bond that draws us into the souls of our
Brothers and Sisters, our Fathers and Mothers, and
Sons and Daughters who are somewhere on this
planet defending our freedom.*

*I know that many of us would take the place of our
loved ones, and I suspect that there are many of
them who would have taken our place on the field
of combat: but as surely as we had our time and
place to defend freedom, they will have theirs.*

*Are we going to send a message of support and love
to our fighting men and women, or are we going to
send a message of hate and discernment. The*

message we send to them now will give them reasons to live. The way we greet them when they return will set the stage of their quality of life for years to come.

Our government says the war in Iraq is over, but our fellow warriors are still there. Please join me in making sure they are not forgotten as we were in Vietnam and so many were in Korea. Please help me to offer them open arms when they return home. Help me to speak out to those who would have our new Heroes bear the burden of decisions made by our politicians. Please remember that war is declared by non-combatants and not the combat soldier.

Thank you and God bless you all.

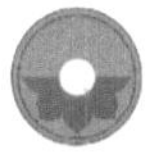

Something I have recently noticed is that I have not experienced any violence, have not had a to be "on guard." The people around me smile all the time. I feel a sense of peace when my sister and brother are about. My lady's voice seems to make everything right and she makes me laugh. And my dad and mother really enjoy my visits. Seeing my children and grandchildren is becoming too important to me. As I sit in God's house and write, I can't help but think that things are too right to be wrong. I will have to see what my sister has to say.

~~ about a moon and a half later ~~

That Man

That man I called Dad is dead.
Only memories left,
And so many words left unsaid,
Another regret.

So missed is he,
And lost do I feel.
My Brother, my Sister
So precious and kind,
And strong.

My Brother sees a lesson,
And my Sister sees an open door.
But I see an emptiness
That will never be filled.

I see a woman left behind,
Who will follow.
But not to soon
I pray.

I see a daughter,
Whose smile holds back tears.
And eyes that
Love her son.

I see silence from two sons,
And disrespect from one,
Selfishness from both,
But my love for them,
Will always be seen.

But this man
I called, "Dad",
Suffers no more
And lives in a better place.

And he lives in the hearts of my Brother,
My Sister, my Daughter,
Mine,
And God's

I Would Take His Place (but of course, I can't)

~~Sometime later (9/9/02)~~

His place I cannot take,
But join him I can,
But what of this message,
And what of my children and theirs?
And my Lady if mine; my friends so few?

As so many of my fellow comrades
Have chosen to end their torment;
Should I?
I think not.

At least not today
Not tonight,
Not this moment, At least not
Until I know what my Sister would say.

My Dad's Life, he said
To my oldest –
Was replaced by her first
And my family's youngest – so beautiful.

I remember a youngest

*I watched grow within
A Mother's body
So young, fragile and frightened.*

*This Mother fought hard,
Fought long,
With courage she fought
To bring this child into the World.*

So thinking of my oldest being brought into this world
by her mother, I cannot help remember another life I
tried to save:

New Death

A village so dirty
And hot and poor,
Lived a child
Soon to have a child.

The medic I delivered
So caring and expert.
To see this child born
Was his only intent.

Set sail on that day,
Medic aboard
Expectations overflowing
And food and clothing to give.

Ashore we went,
And up the path to help.
Up the path went my eyes
To see this child of a child be born.

Scooped up by an enemy's hand,
Smashed into a tree went this newborn,
And his other hand
Ended its Mother's life.

Once again,
My friends: Anger and Hate
Overwhelmed my soul
And my orders were given.

Seconds felt like hours,
And the black clothing
Turned to red
And once again the enemy fell.

Once again
Life for me,
Death for them,
And, ... And I just do not know.

So, Sister, is it so fair that this child and her child should
leave this world with such violence? Is it fair that their
murderers die as a result of your brother's commands,
or his friends of Anger and Hate? What about you,
reader, did I act as a soldier or an executioner?

> *Why, Sister, am I so comfortable with Anger and*
> *Hate,*
> *When my early years were so full of love*
> *And family*
> *And friends?*
>
> *Why, then Sister,*
> *Am I alive and*
> *Those so young are,*
> *At my hand, so dead.*
>
> *Dear God, please help me. I will ring your bell,*
> *clean your house, and guard your servants. I will, I*
> *will, I will, and I will!*
>
> *But I won't, I won't, I won't and can't forget.*
> *But please, please, please help me God.*
>
> *Southward, are you listening?*
>
> *Mr. President, do you care?*

And My Red Riots; do you forgive me?

And in the Southwest: can you help me put this together?

And Mrs. Anderson – pass or fail?

So many years have passed and I am still here. Here beyond what I deserve, but what of that? Who is to say who lives or dies; only God I hope.

By me so hated
Was He.
But today so loved
Is He?

~~Enough tonight, I think. 09/09/02~~

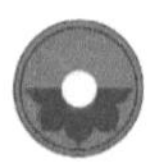

It is time to finish this book. And in two days I will be standing in water with my brother and sister to be baptized. My sister, a woman of the cloth, and my brother, my Father's image, will be with me. She will say the words and he will catch me. God willing, my daughter will be my witness. How is it that a man such as me is being surrounded by people so wonderful?

My sister says, "Being baptized is like a marriage." And I plan not to fail with this marriage. When my sister speaks, you would find it a blessing to listen.

I suspect that I am about to leave a mindly world of violence and hate to go to a spiritual world of love and kindness. I suspect that my heart, now living in two different worlds at the same time, is really coming home, and home to Jesus.

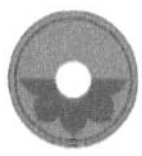

But coming home reminds me of my last days in the
Nam. So many events in only three or four days – please
indulge me:

Four Days

> *Ordered back to Base camp*
> *Ordered to turn my boat*
> *Over to those we*
> *Have protected.*
>
> *To those who*
> *Gave up on their own country.*
> *To those who left their families*
> *To die*
>
> *THREE DAYS*
>
> *Drug tested,*
> *More shots*
> *Clean clothes*
> *And a damn little blue bag.*
>
> *TWO DAYS*

Given our orders,
Departure instructions,
Thinking of
Those left behind.

ONE DAY

Shown where to depart
to watch those
leaving today from that place -
Blown to pieces by an unwelcome mortar.

NO DAYS

Under fire and
On the runway.
Brave chopper pilots
Come for us.

ONE by ONE

We were hoisted into the birds.
Aboard and thinking;
"Safe at last. "

INTO THE AIR

Watching the second chopper
Lifting my friends to safety.
And blown out of the sky.

Fair, I still am not sure. But I know most of you do not know the price of freedom. And I hope freedom does not collect its debt from you. Because your freedom has been paid for.

Few have had the privilege of being God's instruments of peace. Many preach, but few protect God's flock.

God never promised "Fair", just eternal happiness. So I suspect "Is it fair?" is not an issue. So to those of you who feel have been dealt a hand of unfairness, remember that God will make all things right in the end.

And as for me, I say: my ending...

As for me, your author of a lesson in life and a son of a woman that no woman can compare to: Please read and study.

My mother has been an eternal flame in my life. She has never faltered, never turned her back, and has never ever stopped loving me.

I have let her down so many times, as I have my brother, sister, daughter, and my sons. These people worry about me, and for that I gravely feel a burden of sorrow.

But what of sorrow; can I replace my sorrow with other feelings? My sister says love everyone; my brother just does; my mother always has; my daughter has become a teacher of life and love; my sons are still searching.

At fifty-five years, and combat tired and worn out, I search for a reason to go on. Tired, unfair, brutal: yes. But not a lesson for me to pass on. What would my sister say?

How do warriors like us come back to a country that hates us so much? Simple: we keep fighting. We fight and fight and fight; we drink and drink and drink; we drug and drug and drug; and then we cry or die.

Afterword
by Richard's brother

There is little I can say here except to offer some framework. In his last paragraph, Richard lamented about coming back to a country that hated him and others like him. I believe that anger was largely responsible for his pain. He knew it wasn't true, but down in his soul he believed he was hated.

He finished the bulk of this work and put it away about fourteen years before he died. That would be roughly sixteen years before this writing.

The three of us attended our mother's passing. Richard, I think, took it the hardest. He was the most distant as she breathed her last. It was that stare, again. I had the privilege of holding her in my arms. She was an amazing woman and mother.

One day I told her she taught me everything I needed to know about parenting. She "poo-pahed" me and changed the subject. Yep! That was everyone's (4'6") towering nanny. But, back to Richard...

Sometime around 1980 he left Maine and pretty much severed ties with us. He needed a complete geographical change in his life. For him, New Mexico was twenty-two years of normalcy.

After his time in the Southwest, he decided to be near our parents. So, he moved back to Maine. While moving, he spent a few days with us in Massachusetts. It was nice having my big brother nearby for a while.

Around this time my sister was the Senior Pastor at our church in Boston. We thought it would be a nice gesture to have him stay at the church for a bit. He became the resident building manager and stayed about four years.

Oh yeah, while living in the church he met, and fell in love with, our Senior Deacon. One of my most precious memories is the look on his face the moment she took his hand for the first time during a small gathering. After their wedding, they continued living in the church until they found a place of their own in Boston. He didn't make it back to Maine until a little while before his death.

He never left Vietnam memories behind. The guilt ate at him, guilt over what he did in-country and guilt about what he thought he did to us, his family. We all ached to see him whole again. He was a much-loved man, but didn't allow himself the comfort to accept it. During his last few years, I think he allowed himself a little contentment. For that, we're most grateful.

His end was both expected and unexpected.

Sometime after the noon hour on Christmas Day, 2016, he retired for a nap. When a visiting nurse came by to administer his medication, he arose and said he, "...was a little light headed." As he fell back onto the bed he, well...he just stopped.

When our sister called me that afternoon, I knew from the Caller ID exactly what she was going to say. Somehow you know, right?

I suspect it was a nice way to go. His inner turmoil was finally settled. There would be no more days to count.

I love you, Richard. You'll always be my hero.

Near Boston, 2018

After the Afterword

Throughout our conversations, only one of his stories was ever discussed. While finalizing this small book for the printer, I decided to include it here. We talked about it several times, and he always drifted off near the end. He would be soaked in squalid memories and that damn thousand-yard stare would come back.

He had written a poem, in his style, included in the original drafts, but he inexplicably removed it before finishing his story. What follows is my memory of snippets of some of our conversations. This is the only Vietnam experience he personally shared with me in any detail.

As I recall his words:

"Somewhere northwest of our patrol area in the Mekong we were ordered to engage the enemy on land. We were several clicks away from the boat when the enemy discovered us. We were ambushed.

After a brief firefight I was taken prisoner and led away a distance with a rope around my neck. When we stopped for the night, I was put in a bamboo cage.

The cage was poorly built and although my hands were tied, my feet were not. I was able to loosen some of the pieces. When I thought escape was possible, a fight broke out and I was rescued by our people."

Between the one reading of his poem and several conversations, this is what I remembered. I hope it's accurate. I don't recall any details of his escape, the fate of his companions, nor who came to his rescue. I'm not sure whether he ever mentioned the end of the story. The impression I got was that it was his own boat crew with reinforcements, but I don't know for sure. This incident was his most hurtful. Maybe that's why he removed it.

Another deeply held memory was about his daughter.

MJ was born in January 1969 after he had been in Vietnam for about four months. Although not having met her, he adored the idea of having a daughter. As calloused as he had become, he found love in his heart for a little girl he had always wanted.

He saw how little girls were treated in Vietnam and it killed his spirit. He identified with his daughter at every incident.

He thought, as did our father and I, that having a daughter and protecting her from all men was a higher calling. He once told me, "No man wants his daughter to meet someone like us." That's as close a quote as I can remember; we both felt the same way.

Such a paradox, right? You fathers, with crossed fingers, know exactly what I'm saying.

He told me once, "God help the man who's like me." That might have had multiple meanings, but I took it as a reference to his daughter.

He told me he gazed at the moon because the same moon was viewed by his daughter and wife. It was his best connection to home and sanity.

A killer doesn't think like that. He really was a hero.

43

In closing, our sister says, "It's been so long since we've had a good talk, I miss you, Bro. I love you."

– Your sister

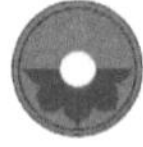 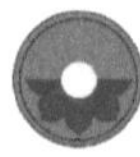 

"Old Reliables"

About Atmosphere Press

Atmosphere Press is an independent, full-service publisher for excellent books in all genres and for all audiences. Learn more about what we do at atmospherepress.com.

We encourage you to check out some of Atmosphere's latest releases, which are available at Amazon.com and via order from your local bookstore:

In the Cloakroom of Proper Musings, a lyric narrative by Kristina Moriconi
Lucid_Malware.zip, poetry by Dylan Sonderman
The Unordering of Days, poetry by Jessica Palmer
It's Not About You, poetry by Daniel Casey
A Dream of Wide Water, poetry by Sharon Whitehill
Radical Dances of the Ferocious Kind, poetry by Tina Tru
The Woods Hold Us, poetry by Makani Speier-Brito
My Cemetery Friends: A Garden of Encounters at Mount Saint Mary in Queens, New York, nonfiction and poetry by Vincent J. Tomeo
Report from the Sea of Moisture, poetry by Stuart Jay Silverman
The Enemy of Everything, poetry by Michael Jones
The Stargazers, poetry by James McKee

About the Author

BUXTON – Richard Lawrence Cleaves, 69, passed away on Sunday, December 25, 2016. He was born on February 23, 1947, in Portland, the son of William E. Cleaves, Jr. and Myrtle (Elliott) Cleaves.

Richard was a graduate of South Port-land High School, Class of 1965, and was Captain of the Cross-Country Team. Following high school, he enrolled at Southern Maine Vocational Technical Institute (1965–1967), where he received his Associate Degree, majoring in Marine Technology.

Richard's proudest accomplishment was serving his country in the U.S. Army 1967–1970. He was a combat veteran in the Vietnam war in the 3rd Battalion, 9th Infantry Division, called "River Raiders." Dad was a boat engineer and gunner during combat. He manned a mounted .50 caliber machine gun, after which he was awarded two Army Commendations with "V" device, and a Bronze Star with "V" device. He was a true American hero!

Richard was known for his kindness, unwavering strength, generosity, and creative side. He never failed to wear a smile, no matter how bad he felt. Most notably in recent years, he honed his skills as a gourmet cook.

He was predeceased by his parents, William E. Cleaves, Jr. and Myrtle E. Cleaves, both of South Portland.

www.ingramcontent.com/pod-product-compliance
Lightning Source LLC
Chambersburg PA
CBHW032131050726
47590CB00008B/3042